View of area in 1939 showing the railroad transfer barges, Holland Tunnel ventilation tower, elevated highway and Canal St. Bridge.

# JAMES BROWN HOUSE
## Ear * Inn * Virons

History of the New York City Landmark and Neighborhood

Est. 1817

by Andrew Coe

ICON SERIES - ODYSSEY PUBLICATIONS

BAR

BEER LIQUOR WINES

RESTAURANT
BAR & GRILL

On a nondescript block of a marginal Manhattan neighborhood, the James Brown House has long made a virtue of its obscurity. For over a century, the only ones who knew the building existed were the dock workers, truckers and garbage men who worked along this gritty strip of the island's lower west side. While the rest of Manhattan was repeatedly torn down and rebuilt in the relentless whirlpool of urban development, the James Brown House remained, gradually decaying and encrusted with the grime of decades, yet still a living storehouse of New York City's legends, myths and history.

The primary neighborhood legend concerns the builder of the house itself, James Brown. City documents merely state that he built the house in 1817; that he sold tobacco and paid his taxes; and that he sold the house in 1833 and then exited from recorded history. A more dramatic story has been passed down by local bootleggers, barflies and long-shoremen: James Brown was of African descent. Born a slave, he became a soldier during the American Revolution and may have served under George Washington. Further, the story goes that on the well-known painting of Washington crossing the Delaware shows, James Brown was the half-seen black soldier pulling oar. Though the painting was made in Germany a half century after the event (the artist likely had no idea of the identity of the participants in the event aside from Washington himself), it is nevertheless possible that Brown could have been there—due to the poor records kept by the Continental Army, we will never really know. The tale continues that Brown received his freedom at the end of the Revolution and, on finally receiving his pension, built his house at 326 Spring Street, living out his days as a local tobacco merchant. In more respectable neighborhoods, these kind of tales have long ago been debunked, paved over and forgotten, but the endurance of the James Brown story on far west Spring Street suggests that beneath all the embellishments lies a grain of truth.

*Opposite: A "lonely survivor": the James Brown House in the 1960s around the time of its Landmarks designation.*

*Below: Dutch style tobacco pipe unearthed in cellar, with model showing its original length. As the pipe clogged with tar, the long end would be broken off until only the bowl remained.*

Emanuel Leutze's "Washington Crossing the Delaware" (1854). This romantic vision of the historical event was painted in a studio in Germany. Photo courtesy of the Metropolitan Museum of Art.

Inset: James Brown may have been similar to this soldier at Washington's knee. The real James Brown will never be known, as most records of free Afro-Americans have been lost.

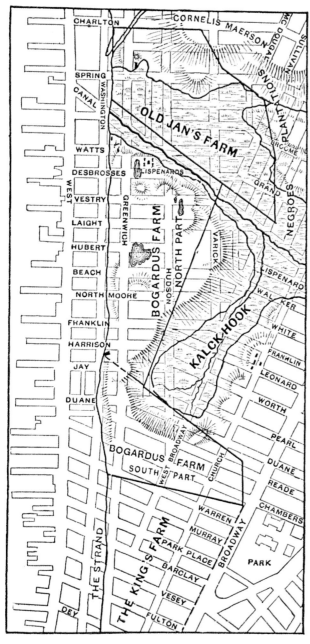

The James Brown House and its legends owe their longevity to the fact that this part of Manhattan Island was never particularly attractive for human habitation. Originally, its location lay just a pace or two from the Hudson River shoreline and at the northern border of a foul-smelling swamp that often flooded at high tide. The swamp's "miasmatic vapors" were said cause deadly "tertian fevers, with their intermediate anguish chills" in anyone living nearby. Colonial New Yorkers preferred the higher and drier ground at the southern tip of Manhattan over a mile to the south, and the city's economic life centered on the sailing ships arriving and departing at the East River docks. The Hudson River side of the island was considered too exposed to the elements for year-round shipping. To make real estate prospects even bleaker, all the land on the west side from Fulton Street up to the village of Greenwich was owned by Trinity Church, which would lease its property but refused to sell it outright, effectively deterring prospective builders.

*Above, left: Map depicting the Colonial farm boundaries overlaid by the modern street grid. The James Brown House is located on the Hudson river boundary of Old Jan's Farm. The King's Farm was later granted to Trinity Church, now the neighborhood's major land owner.*

*Opposite: 1775 map of Manhattan's West Side showing Harrison's Brewery and Lispenard's Farm along the road to Greenwich.*

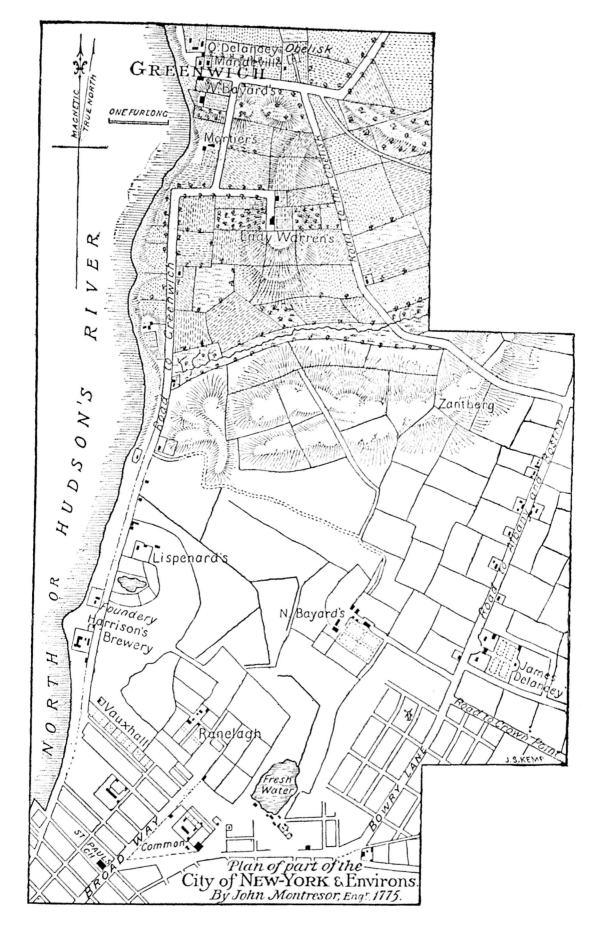

Plan of part of the
City of NEW-YORK & Environs.
By John Montresor, Eng<sup>r</sup>. 1775.

*Above: Hudson view of the North Battery near Hubert St. in the early 1800's.*

*Below: The original Hudson shoreline as per the 'Sanitary Topographic Map' published by the Council of Hygiene and Public Health in 1866.*

S O N

# THE WOMEN OF LISPENARD'S MEADOWS

One of the most intriguing and evanescent legends about the Lower Greenwich neighborhood is the tale of the Jackson Whites. When the British occupied New York during the American Revolution, they had to keep satisfied the thousands of British and Hessian troops billeted here. The story goes that military authorities turned to a man named Jackson, who sailed for England where he either enticed or kidnaped 3,500 British prostitutes. He then packed them in 20 leaky old boats and sailed for the American Colonies. One vessel sank in mid-ocean, so Jackson sent another boat to the West Indies where it picked up a load of replacements, all of African origin. When the prostitutes landed in New York, they were marched to Lispenard's Meadows, where they found a large stockade encircling a group of crude huts that would be their home. When soldiers were ready for fun, they repaired to Lispenard's Meadows and knocked on the stockade door for a few hours with the "Jackson Whites" or the "Jackson Blacks". In 1783, when the British hurriedly evacuated New York, somebody ran to Lispenard's Meadows and unlatched the stockade door, releasing the unfortunate women. About 500 of the prostitutes trekked north up the Hudson, while the remainder somehow crossed the river and, three-thousand-strong, marched west into New Jersey, finally settling in the nearby Ramapo Mountains. They were supposedly the ancestors of a group still living in those hills known as the Jackson Whites or the Ramapo Mountain People.

*Lispenard Meadows in the 18th century. The little stream is now roughly Canal Street.*

The area's slow turnaround began in the 1730s when the seventy-acre swamp was drained to create Lispenard's Meadows, a popular hunting ground for the city elite. The meadows were traversed by the raised causeway of Greenwich Road (now Greenwich Street), which ran up to the village of Greenwich, then a popular summering spot.

On their way north, the city gentry often stopped to drink and dine at Brannon's Garden, a roadhouse at the corner of what is now Spring and Hudson Streets. In 1760, a royal official further helped the area's prospects by building a large mansion, called Richmond Hill, on a rise overlooking the meadows. In 1776, George Washington used Richmond Hill as his headquarters, and after the Revolution, it was home to first Vice President John Adams and then Aaron Burr. By 1800, the area had a name, Lower Greenwich, but only the glimmerings of an urban population.

*Above: Detail of an 1803 map showing Richmond Hill Estate, now Spring Street and Sixth Avenue. The hill was leveled for landfill. The stream flowing from MacDougal Street is Minetta Creek.*

*Left: The Richmond Hill estate house around 1800. This classic Georgian manor house was built in 1760 and was the country estate of the Governor of New York. During the Revolution, the house was headquarters of the British Army under General Gates. George Washington lived here while President before the nation's capital was moved to Philadelphia. Dolly Madison wrote of fox hunting by the river from Richmond Hill. The house was later used as a theater until it burned down in the 1840's*

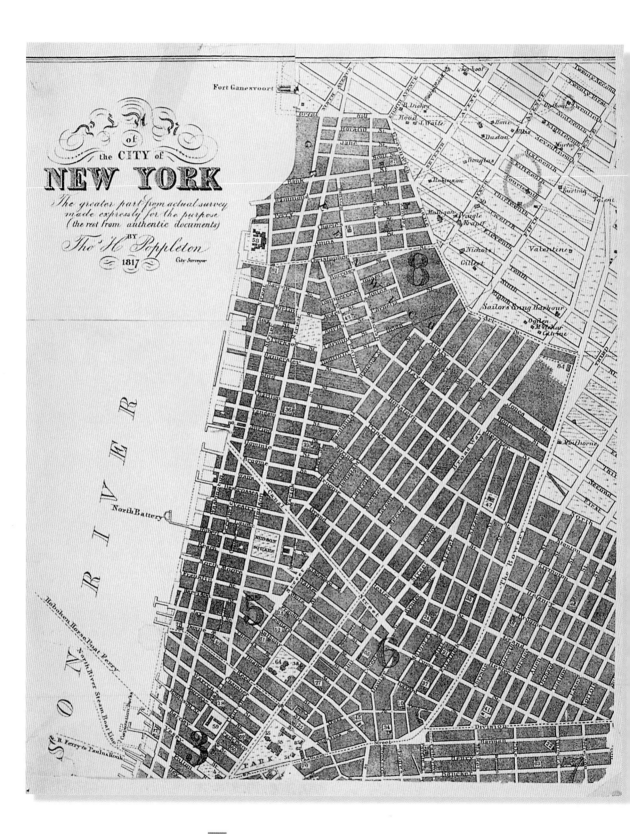

of
the CITY of

# NEW YORK

*The greater part from actual survey
made expressly for the purpose
( the rest from authentic documents)*

BY
*Tho.* H *Poppleton*
1817          *City Surveyor*

The settling of far west Spring Street was encouraged by epidemics and changing real estate economics. In the late eighteenth and early nineteenth centuries, New York was plagued by repeated outbreaks of yellow fever. The government realized that the overcrowded and unsanitary city would only survive if it expanded to the north and west. The city's northbound streets were extended toward the farms and forests of northern Manhattan, and in 1803 Greenwich Village was absorbed into the municipality. Lispenard's Meadows was bisected by a wide canal that drained the Collect Pond (a few blocks north of City Hall) into the Hudson. This waterway was eventually covered over and renamed Canal Street, an important thoroughfare for the area's growth. Along the Hudson River waterfront, Washington Street was extended from the Battery north toward Greenwich Village. By 1807, a street grid overlay the district, and maps noted a landmark on Spring Steet: a public market. The block between Greenwich and Washington Streets was widened to accommodate the 40' by 20' market building, with a cupola holding a bell that rang in the tone of G. In 1810, the city council agreed to build a boat basin at the foot of Spring Street, and within a few years the Hoboken ferry docked here as well as freight boats carrying meat, produce and building materials for the houses that were springing up on every block.

Though most of this area was still owned by Trinity Church, real estate prices in the rest of the city were so high that builders were willing to take a chance on leasing their plots. James Brown was a bit more fortunate, because he was able to purchase his lot outright from the Lispenard family. Unlike many of its leasehold-occupying neighbors, the house has so far held its ground against periodic waves of urban redevelopment. That ground, however, has always been shaky, because building here was a bit like building on Florida swampland. Even today the James Brown House has problems with its foundations. Under its sandstone block footings, the structure stands on sandy mud that has caused it to settle about four feet since 1817, and high tides sometimes fill the basement floor with the water. Luckily

*Opposite: 1817 map showing the ship basin at Spring and Washington Streets that serviced the open-air Clinton market.*

*Below: Timber taken from the attic during reconstruction. Some beams had axe marks and burns, clues that they may have been reused from buildings destroyed during the great fire of 1776.*

*Oyster barges on the Hudson shore. These were often owned by enterprising African-Americans who dug the abundant oysters in New York Harbor.*

the wood frame and floorboards were built of old-growth timber that has held up well. (Some of the beams are charred, indicating that they may have been recycled from buildings burned during the great fire that destroyed much of the city during the Revolution.)

*Above: Buildings along Spring Street in the early 1800s.*

When James Brown built his house here, New York's population of African descent was enjoying a rare opportunity to improve its wealth and status. The state legislature had begun abolishing slavery in 1799, and by 1810 the city was home to over 7,000 free blacks and less than 1,500 slaves. In 1817, an English visitor to the city noted:

> *"One striking feature is the number of blacks, many of whom are finely dressed, the females very ludicrously so, showing a partiality to white muslin dresses, artificial flowers, and pink shoes."*

*Below: Waterfront scene in the late 19th century. This area was the main transit point to Europe and beyond.*

While most free blacks remained in white homes as servants, many others were employed as laborers, artisans, merchants and even professionals. A large fraction of the city's sailors were black; free blacks dominated the oyster

trade; and black artisans worked as carpenters, coopers, cabinetmakers and upholsterers. Blacks found employment in city markets, including presumably the Spring Street Market, mainly as laborers but also in better-paying positions such as butchers and oyster dealers. For those who saved enough to go into business for themselves, a favorite trade was tobacconist, lending credence to the possibility that James Brown was African-American.

In 1817, the block of Spring Street between Greenwich and Washington was full of possibility. Life revolved around the market, which stood in the center of the street itself, with stalls for butchers, fishmongers and produce sellers. The north and south sides of Spring Street were lined with small, brick, Federal-style houses nearly identical to the James Brown House: brick facade, flared lintels above the windows and doors, dormer windows jutting out of the

*A coastal packet schooner docks at Spring Street in the late 1800s.*

*Overleaf: A waterfront tavern in the 1800's. Food was provided free, as long as one drank house brew as well. Then as now, a plethora of nationalities jostled ashore. The bully longshoreman with his hook harasses the Chinaman as the African mediates.*

gambrel roof. Signboards over the doors proclaimed that these were not just homes but places of business occupied by carpenters, booksellers, grocers, marble polishers, tinsmiths and the like. The second and third floors were the family quarters, typically a front and back parlor on the second floor and bedrooms on the third floor. The first floor front was devoted to trade—here James Brown would have sold and stored his tobacco—while the kitchen occupied the back room. A side door in the staircase to the second floor allowed James Brown to step into his shop without going outside. Spring Street was not a particularly quiet or elegant neighborhood, but it perfectly fit the ambitions of those striving to rise to the middle class.

During the 1820s, New York was transformed by far-reaching technological and economic advances. In 1803, Robert Fulton proved that his newly-invented steamboat could successfully travel from the Christopher Street pier all the way to Albany and back. Within two decades, there were forty-three steamboats serving the city and plying the route between New York and Liverpool. Most of them docked on the Hudson side of the island, because the East River piers were still crowded with sailing ships. In 1825, the Erie Canal opened and soon firmly established New York as the nation's preeminent commercial city. Boats filled the harbor and goods crowded the docks. Withing a few short years, far west Spring Street was no longer merely a community marketplace. Landfill had extended the street one

*Left West Side piers in the mid-1800s. The Hudson River was preferred by deep draft steamships, while sailing ships favored the East River docks.*

*Right: View of Spring Street from shipboard. The Greenwich Street elevated train is visible in the distance.*

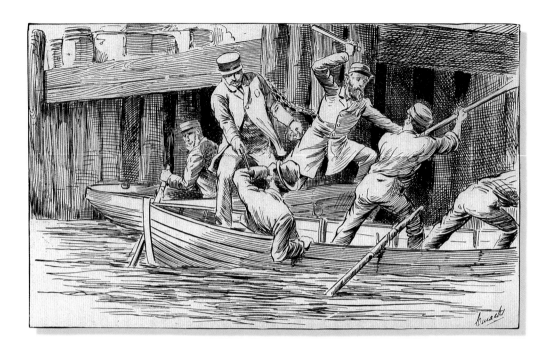

# RIVER PIRATES

## from *"The Gangs of New York"*

by Herbert Asbury, Garden City Publishing Co., 1927

In his report to the Mayor in September 1850, Chief Police George Matsell estimated that there were four to five hundred river pirates in New York, organized in some fifty active gangs. "The river pirates pursue their nefarious operation with the most systematic perseverance, and manifest a shrewdness and adroitness which can only be attained by long practice."

Only one gang of importance operated along the Hudson, a choice collection of ruffians known as the Charlton Street Gang. They made their headquarters in a low gin mill at the foot of Charlton Street and sallied forth each evening to steal whatever was loose upon the docks, and to rob and murder anyone who ventured into their territory. But most of the Hudson River piers were used by ocean going steamers and sailing vessels, and the owners provided well lighted docks and employed a small army of watchmen to guard their property. Consequently the Charlton Street Gang found the pickings very slim, and were at length driven to make a choice between regular piracy and honest labor.

Naturally they chose piracy and roamed the Hudson in rowboats but with scant success until the spring of 1869 when they were joined by a woman known as Sadie the Goat. She obtained her sobriquet because it was her custom, upon encountering a stranger who appeared to possess money of valuable, to duck her head and butt him in the stomach, whereupon her male companions promptly slugged the surprised victim with a slung shot and robbed him at their leisure.

For several years Sadie the Goat was a favorite among the gangsters, but she became embroiled in a fight with Gallus Mag and fled the wad, leaving one of her ears in Gallus Mag's pickling fluid behind the bar of the Hole-in-the-Wall, and sought refuge in the den of the Charlton Street Gang.

Under her inspired leadership, the Gang considerably enlarged their operations, stealing a small sloop of excellent sailing qualities. With the Jolly Roger flying and Sadie the Goat pacing the deck in proud command, they sailed up and down the Hudson robbing farmhouses and riverside mansions, Terrorizing the hamlets and occasionally holding men, women and children for ransom. It has been said that Sadie the Goat, whose ferocity far exceeded that of her ruffianly followers, compelled several men to walk the plank in true piratical style.

For several months the thugs were enormously successful, and filled their hiding places with bales of goods, which they disposed of gradually through fences and junk shops. But after they committed several murders, the embattled farmers along the river began to greet their landing parties with musket and pistol fire and by the end of the summer, life had become so perilous that they abandoned their sloop.

Sadie the Goat is said to have taken her share of the loot and returned to the Fourth Ward, where she made a truce with Gallus Mag who acknowledged her to be the Queen of the Waterfront. Gallus Mag was so touched be the abject surrender of her erstwhile rival that she dipped into her jar of trophies and returned one female ear to its original owner. Legend has it that Sadie the Goat had her ear enclosed in a locket and wore it about her throat.

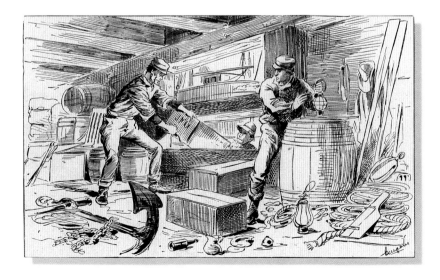

*Below: Pump on Greenwich Street, below Canal.*

block west to the new waterfront thoroughfare of West Street. The little market building had been replaced by the Clinton Market, a large municipal structure on the block bounded by Spring, Washington, Canal and West Streets, which received its produce at a new deepwater pier extending into the Hudson. The Lower Greenwich neighborhood was developing into one of the many spokes of the mighty trading power that was New York.

The change came not without a price. Uncertain about employment and faced with competition from new immigrant groups, young artisans and apprentices turned to mob action, sometimes to force political or economic change but often merely to vent their frustrations. The first sign of this unrest on Spring Street was the appearance of a youth gang in 1825:

> *There is a knot of young men who reside in the neighborhood of Spring Street, who style themselves the Spring Street Fencibles and who have long been a terror to the inhabitants residing in that quarter. They assemble at their different haunts or porter houses, in the evening, where they arrange their plans, get well primed, and sally out in squads to regulate the city. Nor are they very particular who they assault, often knocking down black females, and then, when the watch is called, separate and dodge round a corner, until things become quiet, when, by a concerted signal, they come together again, compare notes, chuckle, and boast how they gave it to her in the bread-basket.*

One night, after drinking many glasses of beer, gin and brandy, they came upon a party of gentlemen, whom they first taunted and then physically attacked. During the battle, a Spring Streeter killed Henry Lambert, one of the city's leading businessmen. The newspapers bemoaned the fact that a group of young apprentices would spend their nights carousing and fighting: "These things were not so in former times." Unfortunately, from now on mob violence would not be the exception but the rule.

In 1833, James Brown sold his house at 326 Spring Street to James Lewis and Bayard Blachly, who ran a nearby apothecary shop. In retrospect, it was a good time for a black merchant to sell his business, especially on Spring Street. Most of the area's blacks worshiped at the Spring Street Presbyterian Church (over at the corner of Varick Street) whose pastor, Henry Ludlow, was a prominent supporter of the abolition of slavery. The abolitionists were in the minority in the New York of that era. Many white New Yorkers feared that blacks were becoming too strong and self-sufficient and that their economic power would lead to competition for work and, even worse in some minds, racial intermingling. These fears were particularly strong among the new immigrants from Ireland, who moved into neighborhoods like the Five Points district that already had large black populations. In July of 1834, fanned by racist diatribes in two local newspapers, white working class mobs began attacking black-owned businesses, black passers-by and the homes and churches of abolitionist preachers. When they arrived at the Spring Street church, they burst through the doors and destroyed the interior, then using the shattered pews to build barricades on the street outside in anticipation of a battle with national guardsmen. Afterward, many whites blamed the riots on black demands, not white rioters, and over the next decades, blacks faced increasing discrimination in nearly every phase of their lives.

In the 1840s and 1850s, far west Spring Street began its transformation from a residential neighborhood to one

*Civil War era view of Spring and Canal Streets. This scene shows the embarkation of the Fire Zouaves heading off to battle the Confederate army. A volunteer regiment made up largely of firemen, the Fire Zouaves were modeled after the French Foreign Legion army in Algeria, who in turn took the name and elegant costume from the Zouaoua people native to the area. Their distinctive uniforms, made up of gray jackets, gray flowing trousers and red firemen's shirts, were so popular that thousands more clamored to join this regiment.*

*Above: 1867: Charles Harvey demonstrates the first elevated railway line, constructed along Greenwich Street and 9th Avenue between Dey and 20th Streets.*

centered around the shipping industry. Number 326 remained property of the Lewis family, meat and provisions dealers, who lived around the corner and rented out the floors to local craftsmen and workers and their families. Half a block west, the Clinton Market was waning in importance as the increasingly centralized food distribution business gravitated to the much larger Washington Market downtown. At the Canal Street pier docked the huge trans-Atlantic steamers of the Collins Line, considered marvels of American engineering know-how. Spring Street smaller pier received local freight and provision boats and provided semi-permanent berths for all kinds of floating businesses, including warehouses, oyster vendors and coal suppliers. More warehouses lined West Street and even began to appear on the formerly residential blocks of Washington Street. Lower Greenwich became part of the unbroken stretch of docks and ships that lined the city's Hudson waterfront:

The shore front from the Battery northward along the Hudson differed greatly from that of the East River. Instead of the forests of masts which rose there, the Hudson for some distance was crowded with funnels. Instead of sailing-vessels, steamers were in the slips, as varied in their classes and sizes as they were in their destinations. Ferry-boats sailed to Jersey City and Hoboken; steamers traveled between the city and towns up the Hudson; larger boats sailed to Newport, Allyn's Point and Stonington, where they connected with railway lines for Boston. Still further up the river, lay the tugs, some employed to tow the sea-going craft to and from the harbor; others to tow sloops, barges, and schooners up and down the river. The upper slips were occupied by barges and the smaller sailing craft engaged in the river trade. The quays here, as on the East River shore, were lined with rows of warehouses, and towards the upper end of the city factories made their appearance.

*Below: White Rose wagon making a delivery to the James Brown House about 1910.*

PLATE 3.

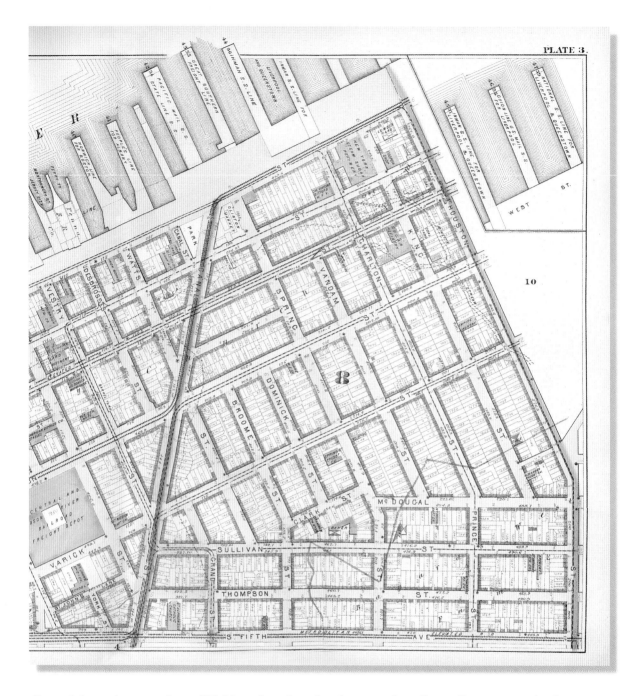

*Above: Osborne insurance lot map of 1924. Clinton Market still stood at the end of Spring St. just north of Canal St. Park. Note the railroad tracks on Canal St. and original water line marks.*

Within a few decades the ceaseless flow of commerce had utterly remade the neighborhood. Spring Street echoed with the clatter of hooves, the roar of wagon wheels on cobblestones and the shouts of workingmen as millions and millions of dollars in goods moved between the Hudson River piers and the city every day. The Pacific Mail

Steam Ship Company sailing to California, Japan and China docked at the improved Spring Street pier, while along West Street chugged the locomotives of the New York Central pulling long freight trains. On Greenwich and Washington Streets the tracks of the 9th Avenue Street Horse Car Rail Road. As merchants and businessmen found homes elsewhere, their houses were replaced by stables, lumberyards, sugar refineries, slaughterhouses, coal yards, brick yards, iron foundries and warehouses. East of Greenwich Street, the blocks remained largely residential, but from Greenwich west to the water, industry and commerce now held sway. For those residents that remained, the quality of the neighborhood began to spiral down, following reformer Jacob Riis's observation that *"gashouses, slaughterhouses and the docks, that attract the roughest crowds and support the vilest saloons, invariably form slum centers."*

*Above: A neighborhood gang in the 1940s.*

*Below: Longshoreman's hook, used for handling cargo and enforcing discipline.*

*Below: Canal Street between Varick and Hudson Streets facing the Greenwich Street el to the west.*

Indeed, the area around the Clinton Market became part of a waterfront strip of "many squalid homes, many vile saloons, and...much dirt and ignorance." One of the area's worst blocks was the James Brown House's own, whose squalor rivaled the Lower East Side. Here landlords had constructed a warren of tenement apartment buildings to attract the recent immigrants, mainly Irish, who found back-breaking jobs on the nearby waterfront. Though sorely lacking in schools, playgrounds and Catholic churches, the neighborhood did have plenty of bars: "The dramshop yawns at every step, the poor man's club, his forum and his haven of rest when weary and disgusted with the crowding, the quarreling, and the wretchedness at home." And, like many Manhattan slums, the block even had its own gang that terrorized the community during the 1880s:

> The "Boodle Gang"...was located principally in a nest of double tenement houses on the block bounded by Greenwich, Washington, Spring and Canal Streets. These buildings made up a perfect hive of thieves, and it numbered many expert garroters. It made forays up to the market-men of Central Market, and on the provision wagons which passed through their neighborhood.

The Lower West Side slums became an issue during the 1890s, when a group of urban reformers began attacking horrendous conditions in the tenement district. One of its major targets was Trinity Church, which owned over 300 tenement buildings, some housing saloons and opium dens, from Greenwich Street east to Sullivan Street. Seeing church properties purely as investments, Trinity's managers refused to make basic improvements like running water on each floor and lights in the hallways. When it was revealed that Trinity's tenants had higher death rates than the city average, the furor led to passage of the Tenement House Bill mandating a whole series of basic changes in tenement construction and operation. Rather than make these improvements, however, Trinity's property managers preferred to tear down their residential buildings and lease the lots to businesses looking for industrial space. Large factories and industrial loft buildings quickly rose on Spring Street, dwarfing the few remaining 19th century homes in the neighborhood.

In the early 1890s, an Irish immigrant named Thomas Cloke decided that a gritty block of Spring Street was worth an investment. He rented and later purchased 326 Spring Street and Number 324 next door. Cloke was an immigrant success story; he had arrived in the United States only a decade or two earlier, and already he was living with his family on a respectable block in Greenwich Village. Cloke's business was selling beer and liquor to ships, and he bought the James Brown House because of its perfect location near the docks, beginning the building's century-long association with alcohol. Cloke and his brother Patrick bottled corn whiskey in the basement and manufactured beer in a small

CANAL 6-9060

## Cloke Bar & Grill
### Restaurant
BEER, WINES AND LIQUOR
*KNOWN FROM COAST TO COAST*

326 SPRING STREET
NEW YORK CITY

## A SOUVENIR OF NEW YORK'S LIQUOR INTERESTS
AMERICAN PUBLISHING AND ENGRAVING COMPANY, NEW YORK, 1893.

Produced for the 1893 Columbian Exposition in Chicago, this book contains descriptions of around 400 Manhattan alcohol wholesalers, retailers, bars, restaurants and hotels.

### Excerpt

**THOS. CLOKE & CO., Wholesale Liquor Dealers, No. 326 Spring Street.**
Among the many excellent and trustworthy houses in the wholesale branch of this line, especial attention is directed to the establishment of Messrs. Thomas Cloke & Co., located at the above address, with a branch house at No. 204 East One Hundred and Twentieth Street. They are direct receivers of all the leading brands of whiskies from the prominent producing centers, and few houses have the facility and ability to exercise better taste in the selection of prime stock than is possessed by them. Mr. Cloke is a middle-aged gentleman, born in Ireland, and a resident of the United States for about twenty-three years. Though only established since 1888, Mr. Cloke can point with justifiable pride to a thriving business of enviable proportions. He has ten men in his employ, and keeps in stock a very complete line of all varieties and grades of wines and liquors, which are the best value in the city for the moderate prices asked. The main part of the trade is done in the city and surrounding country, and goods are sold either in bulk, in bottle or case lots. Mr. Cloke is also an extensive dealer in the best grades of China, Japan and India teas, and choice domestic cigars. The trade in these lines forms an important item in the aggregate of the business. Cigars are sold in no smaller lots that five hundred, and from that figure up to any amount that is ordered. The brands offered are faithfully maintained at the highest standard of excellence, and for fine flavor, finish and quality, challenge comparison with any similar goods in the market. Mr. Cloke is an experienced man, standing in the highest esteem with the business world for his energy, ability and probity.

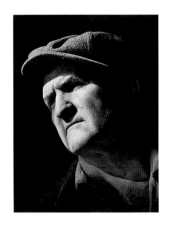

*Above: A longshoreman awaiting work on the waterfront.*

*Opposite: 1893 temperance poster, typical of the advocacy that led to Prohibition.*

*Below: Stanley the sailor and shipwright of the Ear under the glass of a submarine porthole. Painting by John Paul.*

brewery filling the old backyard. The first floor of 326 Spring became a "public" bar where food was also served. It was the closest saloon to the waterfront, and, according to local legend, the moment a ship pulled into the nearby docks the passengers and crew would immediately head for Spring Street and line up at Cloke's door. For four decades a sign saying "Thomas Cloke Liquor" hung over the door. Cloke became a respected member of the neighborhood in the tradition of the community "publican" of the Old Country.

Cloke's principal customers were dock workers and the drivers who transported the goods on and off the piers. The dock workers were divided into to three social classes: longshoremen, coastwise workers and "shenangoes." The elite were the longshoremen, almost all Irish, who handled all the big ships coming from foreign points and earned upward of 25 cents an hour. In 1915, one writer gave a somewhat romanticized description of this breed:

> *A clean-cut man nearly fifty years of age, clean shaven save his upper lip, five feet nine in height, and weighing about 170 pounds, broad in the shoulders, strong of arm, but with a slight stoop; somehow wholesome looking, a man that one would touch without recoil, notwithstanding the accumulation of cargo dirt; a man who supports a wife and four children and inhabits a four-room tenement; a man who speaks in a high-pitched voice suggestive of much loud shouting, and laughs with a deep reverberating laugh indicating friendliness and good-fellowship; a hearty eater and lover of a social drink with his companions; a friendly man throughout, but a quick, keen critic of his fellow-workman; thoroughly efficient in all the details of his own work, and surprisingly full of information concerning the matters and methods of the waterfront.*

# HARDACRE'S TEMPERANCE MAP ILLUSTRATING THE
# EFFECT OF ALCOHOLIC DRINKS AND NARCOTICS ON THE HUMAN SYSTEM.

The Healthy.

The moderate drinker.

The chronic drunkard.

In Delirium.

Plate I. A healthy stomach.

Plate II. A stomach after ten or fifteen days continuous drinking.

Plate III. Last stages of ulcerated stomach of chronic drunkard.

Stomach Showing
Plate IV. Last stages of Delirium Tremens.

Plate V. Healthy brain.

Plate VI. Effects of alcohol upon brain.

Plate VII. A healthy liver.

Plate VIII. Contracted or "hob-nail" liver.
Cause—Continuous use of Alcohol.

Plate IX. Healthy Lung.

Plate X. Chronic Bronchial Catarrh from use of alcohol

Plate XI. Fatty degeneration and enlargement of Liver. Cause—Too much stimulant.

Plate XII. Healthy Heart.

Plate XIII. Fatty Degeneration of the Heart

Plate XIV. Healthy Kidney.

Plate XV. Contracted or "Spirit Kidney."

Plate XVI. Fatty Degeneration and enlargement of Kidney.

Plate XVII. Effects of a few glasses of intoxicants upon intestines.

Plate XVIII. Inflammation of intestines, the result of use of alcohol.

1. Healthy Artery. 2. Artery dilated by alcohol.
Plate XIX.
Effect of alcohol upon Arteries. 3. Weakened wall of Artery rupture from long continued distention.

Plate XX. Ulceration of intestines from chronic alcoholism.

Plate XXI. Effect upon the intestines of Delirium Tremens.

Plate XXII. A Manly Boy.

Plate XXIII. An Emaciated Youth, whose exalted ambitions have fled—A Cigarette Fiend.

Plate XXIV. Portion of Lung showing deposit of Nicotine in air cells from Cigarette smoking. Boy 17 years of age.

Plate XXV. Healthy Blood Corpuscles.

Plate XXVI. Blood Corpuscles destroyed by alcohol.

Plate XXVII. Tobacco Cancer caused by smoking.

Plate XXVIII.
Where Many a Workingman's Money Goes

The average laboring man spends about fifty cents a day for tobacco, beer and whiskey—fifty cents for seven years amounts to a sum large enough to buy a neat little home and furnish it.

The average laboring man spends more money for tobacco, beer and whiskey than he does for what he eats and wears.

Annual consumption of liquors in the United States, 1,184,000,000 gallons.
Annual consumption of liquors per capita in the United States, 19.75 gallons.
Annual expenditure for liquors in the United States, $1,200,000,000.00.

Annual expenditure per capita in the United States, $20.00.
Annual number of deaths from alcohol, 100,000.
Number of habitual drunkards in the United States, 650,000.

Per cent of alcohol contained in each of the following drinks:

| | Per Cent. | | Per Cent. |
|---|---|---|---|
| Cider, | 5 to 10 | Tansy, | 40 to 50 |
| Lager Beer, | 5 | Brandy, | 50 to 54 |
| Ale, | 5 to 20 | Whiskey, | 45 to 55 |
| Wine, | 8 to 22 | Proof Spirit, | 49 |
| Gin, | 40 to 50 | Bitters, | 5 to 6 |

Half the idiots in the world are the children of drunkards. More than half the insanity is due to alcohol, while it produces four out of every five of our paupers and nine out of every ten of the criminals with which our prisons are crowded, and the misery and wretchedness which it brings not only upon those who use it, but upon their parents, wives and children lie beyond calculation.

PUBLISHED BY F. G. L. RACE

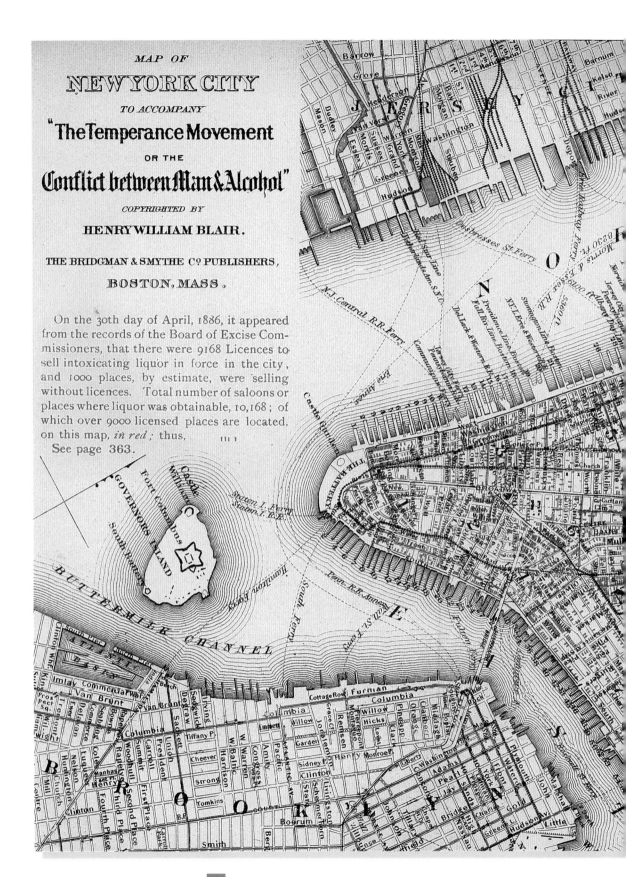

MAP OF

# NEW YORK CITY

*TO ACCOMPANY*

## "The Temperance Movement

### OR THE

## Conflict between Man & Alcohol"

*COPYRIGHTED BY*

### HENRY WILLIAM BLAIR.

THE BRIDGMAN & SMYTHE Cº PUBLISHERS,

BOSTON, MASS.

On the 30th day of April, 1886, it appeared from the records of the Board of Excise Commissioners, that there were 9168 Licences to sell intoxicating liquor in force in the city, and 1000 places, by estimate, were selling without licences. Total number of saloons or places where liquor was obtainable, 10,168; of which over 9000 licensed places are located, on this map, *in red;* thus,

See page 363.

*Above: Longshoremen shaping up for work on the West Side docks.*

*Italian hand-blown wine jug from the mid-1800s, dug up during cellar excavations.*

Below the longshoremen came the coastwise workers, who loaded and unloaded goods, mainly lumber, from the smaller freight boats that plied the nation's Atlantic ports. Finally, at the bottom were the shenangoes, waterfront drifters, mainly alcoholics, who picked up odd jobs here and there. Every morning, the dock workers would arrive at the pier entrance for the 6:30 a.m. "shape-up." They would form a semicircular line, in front of which the foreman would pace selecting men for the day's labor, which usually lasted ten hours or more. They could carry sacks full of flour, salt or birdseed, or sides of beef, weighing upward of 300 pounds; or they could work in the hold while heavy machinery was lowered down on cables that could snap in an instant. Accidents were frequent and

*Above: Corner of Hudson Street and Canal Street in 1905*

deaths a common occurrence. Some longshoremen got work nearly every day while many others worked less than half the time. Rather than go home, they preferred to idle away the hours at taverns like Thomas Cloke's:

> *They can not go to their homes for fear they will not be on hand when wanted. Consequently, they must stand on the sidewalks, in doorways, or on street corners and acquire the reputation of being loafers; or go to the saloon which is always conveniently located, and be stamped as drunkards. For it is impossible to remain in the saloon and take nothing. The man who does not drink is asked with intent, "Who is paying the rent?" or "Who pays for these lights?" He must drink or leave. Given the*

*alternative of standing room on the street or in a saloon, does the ordinary workman hesitate if he can afford the latter? And if the argument for the saloon is convincing in fair weather, how much more is it unanswerable in extreme heat, extreme cold, rain, or snow?*

In 1919, the 18th Amendment to the Constitution, better known as the Prohibition Law, was enacted. Rather than defy the law, as so many would so profitably do, Cloke decided it was time to get out. He leased the business to John Rolandi (though the sign still said "Thomas Cloke Liquor") and retired to Queens. The business now claimed to be merely a restaurant, but behind curtain was the entrance to a backroom speakeasy, one of the thousands that peppered

Manhattan during Prohibition. One veteran pub-crawler describes the type:

> "The humble bar-room with its sawdust-splashed floor, modeled on saloon lines, smacks of pre-war days. It flaunts a bar, with foot-rail and cuspidors and, as of yore, contains a back room. The patronage is mainly masculine, the air reeks of tobacco smoke, and he who starts to get tough is promptly ejected by a pair of expert bouncers. All in all, a poor place to go looking for trouble. For the next five decades, the bar was associated with the small-scale criminality of the rough-and-tumble waterfront world."

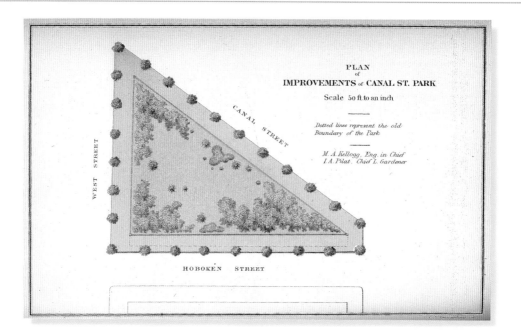

PLAN
of
IMPROVEMENTS of CANAL ST. PARK

Scale 50 ft.to an inch

Dotted lines represent the old
Boundary of the Park

M.A.Kellogg, Eng. in Chief
I.A.Pilat, Chief L.Gardener

CANAL STREET

WEST STREET

HOBOKEN STREET

*Plan of 1877 for Canal St. Park. This triangle on the river shore was once used for dockage on the Canal and a market ground for goods laid off ships. It later became a flower market and when the area was residential in the early 1800's, a neighborhood park. When the Holland Tunnel was constructed in the 1920's, the land was appropriated for highway lanes. Until 2000 the park was used as City Sanitation Department equipment parking lot. By research and advocacy of neighbors, the land was reclaimed for the City Parks Depatment and rebuilt as a riverside park.*

That same year, the New York and New Jersey Vehicular Tunnel Commission decided to dig a tunnel from Manhattan under the Hudson River to Jersey City. An engineer named Clifford Holland designed the two tubes of the tunnel, which were excavated using the radical new "shield" method. A steel cylinder was driven into the rock, while workmen known as sandhogs removed the rubble from its center. The city demolished the moribund Clinton Market, and in 1922 workers began digging the first tube of the tunnel starting at the intersection of Canal and West Streets. A year later, construction of the second tube began at West and Spring Streets, digging through centuries of fill and garbage before hitting bedrock. A large structure rose on the southwest corner of Spring and Washington Streets housing maintenance equipment and the tunnel's ventilation ducts.

For four years, heavy equipment, trucks and dirt filled the neighborhood; many of the remaining residents fled as their buildings were condemned to make way for tunnel construction and replacement of the water mains. Number 326 was saved, probably because it stood on a private lot (not leasehold) and housed a bar where tunnel workers slaked their thirst, making it too profitable to sell. Instead, the Holland Tunnel engineers protected it from the vibrations by installing new columns and beams to prop up the building's frame. The Holland Tunnel finally opened on November 13, 1927. Its actual entrance was a few blocks to the south west, but the new flows of traffic along Canal and Varick Streets in effect isolated the neighborhood from the surrounding district.

Almost every commentator ranked the newly-opened Holland Tunnel as the eighth wonder of the world. The sole dissenting voice came from the sophisticates at the New Yorker:

> *"No victory was ever more hollow than the success of the new Holland tunnel. You approach it with eagerness, you drive through it with speed and eclat, you emerge at the other end with joy and thanksgiving. And then where are you? In Jersey City!"*

The West Side piers in the 1920's with the Hamburg Line docks across the Hudson River.

The tunnel's construction forever altered the character of far west Spring Street. Between 1920 and 1930, the neighborhood lost about half its population. In 1920, most of the block's residents were the sons and daughters of Irish immigrants, with also a few Portuguese immigrants and Italian families. The men and women were mostly laborers of one kind or another, working on the docks, in factories, or in local stables. By 1930, most of the families were gone. Spring Street was home mostly to single men, the vast majority of them longshoremen and sailors. In the 1930 census, the majority of residents identified themselves as U.S. born to American parents, followed by Portuguese and Irish immigrants and one Italian family. Over the next decades, even this population would dwindle, until only a handful of people lived on the block.

Below: Frame houses under the el on the north side of Spring and Greenwich Streets, now the site of the UPS terminal.

During the Depression, the neighbor hood witnessed one last, brief-lived population explosion. Hundreds of home- less men and women built a "hobo jungle" on the large vacant lot left by tunnel construction on the north side of Spring Street between Washington and West Streets. Relatively concealed from the rest of the city, they erected little huts out of cast-off timber and sheet metal and lasted a year or two before the government finally cleared them off. Whenever one of the homeless men would come into the Cloke Bar & Grill, the bartender would always give them a bowl of soup on the house.

*The Holland Tunnel entrance in 1930.*

The 1939 WPA guidebook to New York City described a Hudson River waterfront that on the surface was not much different from thirty or even fifty years earlier:

> *The broad highway, West Street, and its continua- tions, which skirts the North River from Battery Place to Fifty-ninth Street, is, during the day, a surg- ing mass of back-firing, horn-blowing, gear-grind- ing trucks and taxis. All other waterfront sounds are submerged in the cacophony of the daily ava-*

*lanche of freight and passengers in transit....South of Twenty-third Street, the river is walled by an almost unbroken line of bulkhead sheds and dock structures....Opposite the piers, along the entire length of the highway, nearly every block houses its quota of cheap lunchrooms, tawdry saloons and waterfront haberdasheries catering to the thousands of polyglot seamen who haunt the "front." Men "on the beach" (out of employment) usually make their headquarters in barrooms, which are frequented mainly by employees of the lines leasing piers in the vicinity.*

*Below: Depression era "Hooverville" on Spring Street and West Street during the 1930s (now the site of the UPS terminal).*

The great change, however, was that, aside from a few retired sailors, fewer and fewer people lived here. Spurred by the relentless vision of Robert Moses, the old mixed-use neighborhoods (like Lower Greenwich) accommodating

homes, shops and markets were destroyed. From now on, residential and industrial zones would be separated, linked only by a network of modern highways. Many of the remaining nineteenth-century buildings on the Lower West Side were torn down to make way for factories and industrial loft buildings. Above West Street, the Miller Elevated Highway (later renamed the West Side Highway) ran from the Battery all the way up to the Bronx. Instead of having to fight their way through the waterfront traffic jams, drivers could speed their way above them. Shortly after World War II, all the old buildings on the north side of Spring Street between Greenwich and Washington were demolished to make way for the enormous Union Terminal Freight Station. The piers and ships became attractions to view from the comfort of their automobiles, no longer integral to city life.

*Below: A neighborhood home-steader during the Depression.*

The culture of the docks became increasingly isolated, inward-looking and self-destructive. Now power on the waterfront was in the hands of the International Longshoremen's Association (ILA). Rather than protect their workers, the ILA bosses operated in league with organized crime to steal everything they could from both the docks and longshoremen's pockets. The shipping companies did not mind as long as thefts were kept within reason and cargo kept moving. The ancient shape-up system continued, but now under the control of the union, giving them nearly total power over the lives of the workers. In addition to union dues, longshoremen were required to make "voluntary contributions" to their foremen, borrow money from organization loan sharks and, above all, keep their mouths shut about anything that happened on the docks. Union dissidents were labeled "communists" and faced swift and violent reprisals. Waterfront murders were common and rarely reported to the police—the victims merely "fell off" the pier.

The Lower West Side piers were controlled by Eddie McGrath and John "Cockeye" Dunn, both ILA officials operating out of the Christopher Street local. McGrath and Dunn were intimate friends of mob bosses Joey Adonis and Meyer Lansky, as well as numerous corrupt local politicians and policemen. To run their piers, they hired dozens of known criminals, including murderers just out of prison, and probably earned millions for themselves, the mob and the officials they paid off. In 1947, Dunn and Andrew "Squint" Sheridan murdered a hiring stevedore on the Greenwich Village docks for failing to follow orders, a crime for which both received the death sentence. Closest to Spring Street, on Piers 34 and 36 (of the New York and Cuba Mail Steamships of the Ward Line) McGrath and Dunn ran a lucrative numbers racket among the dock workers and oversaw the constant pilferage of goods being loaded and unloaded. Perishable fruits like bananas often landed at Pier 34, where the pier bosses perfected the art of work slowdowns until the shippers paid them off to prevent the fruit from going bad. The pervasive crime and

*Top left: The waterfront in the 1940s with the ferry "Binghamton," now a floating restaurant in Edgewater New Jersey.*

*Below: Area in the 1940's showing busy piers and the growth of industrial buildings around the Holland Tunnel.*

*Above: A five-round revolver found in the House chimney, perhaps hidden there from police.*

*Opposite: The James Brown House in 1973.*

corruption on the docks lasted through the 1950s. In 1953, the outcry surrounding the Waterfront Commission investigation forced the resignation of ILA president Joseph Ryan, but the union remained as entrenched as ever.

During this era, the bar at 326 Spring Street remained one of those "tawdry saloons" favored by local workers. In 1956, John Rolandi, who had bought the building from Thomas Cloke's daughter back in the 1930s, sold out to Ethel Nussdorf, who changed the name to Nussdorf's Bar & Grill. It was longshoreman's joint, and waterfront-related rackets clearly thrived in its back room. It opened at 6 a.m. and did its peak business between six and eight in the morning among the workers who had not been hired at the shape-up. In the back room, which still had a curtain drawn over its entry, they could cash their paychecks, buy stolen merchandise, place numbers and horse-racing bets and take out loans from the resident loan shark. The upstairs, which was divided into small rooms, was at times a brothel for visiting sailors. By early afternoon most of its customers had done their business, drunk their fill and the bar closed for the day.

During the 1950s and 1960s, the bar followed the waterfront down. The old methods of shipping in crates were rapidly being replaced by the new methods of containerization, and there was simply not enough room on the west side for the huge cranes needed to unload container ships. New, modern docks were built across the harbor at the Port of Newark, while other modernized harbors like Baltimore began to aggressively compete for New York's business.

BEER LIQUOR WINES

Rheingold
EXTRA DRY

PUSH

326

*Below: The James Brown house in 1973 with the Archibald & Kendall spice packing warehouse which once covered the neighborhood with pungent aromas.*

Passengers, meanwhile, preferred to travel by air. The shipping companies went out of business; the docks one were abandoned and began to sag into the river; and New York City waterfront, once one of the wonders of the modern world, slowly fell silent. During the 1950s, 48,000 dock workers worked around the Port of New York; by 1985, there were only 12,000. At 326 Spring Street, the same old patrons propped themselves up at the bar every day, grad-

ually drinking themselves to death, but one by one they disappeared and nobody showed up to take their place.

In 1963, the demolition of the Roman-style old Pennsylvania Station building sparked the beginning of the city's historic preservation movement. Two years later, the Landmarks Preservation Commission was founded to preserve as many historically or aesthetically important buildings as possible. The commission immediately began a survey of all five of the city's boroughs, looking not only for old buildings but for structures that were important at each stage of the city's development. One of these was the small, early 19th century house: "the most pleasing and artistic pattern of habitation New York has ever known." In 1964, the architecture critic Ada Louise Huxtable wrote:

*Where, now, are the houses of yesteryear? Surprisingly, many are still with us–in side streets, in slums slated for the bulldozer, scattered through the lower tip of the island, near the rivers, hidden behind skyscrapers, jammed between newer neighbors, painted, remodeled, refaced, disguised, disfigured, ignored. They have been enlarged, made smaller, cut in half, supplied with signs and shop windows, converted to storage, fish houses, barber shops and bars. Occasionally "restored," frequently "modernized," the ravages are always equally severe. Few New Yorkers are aware that the comfortable, charming, and historically important small house c. 1800-30 still exists. It is too well hidden, too efficiently defaced, and– above all- -too fast disappearing.*

*Left: Can of "Arctic Lunch" brand tomatoes found in the attic eaves.*

*Below: Old shoe found in a House wall. Single shoes were put into buildings under construction for good luck.*

In 1966, while strolling among the industrial buildings and garages that lined the Lower West Side, Landmarks Preservation Commission staffers stumbled upon 326 Spring Street. After 149 years, the first floor, which was originally up a flight of steps from the street, had sunk to the level of the sidewalk. The building was listing to one side, and the facade had been painted dark green. The first-floor saloon was only marked by a red neon "BAR" sign above the door and another sign "BEER LIQUOR WINES" across the front window. Patrons simply referred to it as the "Green Door," and its manager was sullen and uncommunicative

The sodden barflies may not have realized it, but they were sitting in an historical gem. According to the preservation movement leader Harmon Goldstone, it was a "lonely survivor," a "reminder that people actually once lived here." In 1969, the Landmarks Preservation Commission designated 326 Spring Street a landmark:

> *The James Brown House is a modest example of an early nineteenth century Federal house with some of its original architectural features, that after one hundred and fifty years, it is still serving a useful purpose and that it adds charm, intimate scale, a provocative change of pace to our city life and scene."*

Recognition as a landmark, however was no guarantee that the James Brown House would be preserved. The Nussdorf family had leased the structure to Harry Jacobs, a Hungarian immigrant who managed the bar but seemed to have little hope in the future of either the building or the neighborhood. It was rumored that the late nineteenth-century tenement building next door was going to be razed, and Jacobs was sure that number 326 would collapse along with it. Despite prodding from the Landmarks Commission, Jacobs refused to do any work to return the facade to its original design or even begin any structural repairs. It somehow suited his bleak view of the bar, his drunken patrons and the gritty, half-abandoned streets outside just to watch the building slowly fall down around him.

During the 1960s, the shabby rooms above the Green Door bar were home to a retired sailor named Mickey who repaired radios and televisions. One day he stepped out onto Spring Street to feed pidgeons and was run over. His ghost is still heard and felt in the James Brown House, a friendly, if sad presence.

*Above: James Browns' shop window cover, a protective panel typical of 18th Century shops. A bird painting from 1979 by David Wirt graces the original shop window cover.*

The 1970s were a nadir both for the City in general and for the Lower West Side. Not only were the docks empty and obsolete but West Side Highway had to be condemned after a garbage truck fell through a pothole and landed in the Gansevoort Market. The only businesses that were active on far west Spring Street were the garbage companies parked their trucks in the neighborhood garages and vacant lots and used the streets as open-air waste sorting plants. At nights and on weekends, the area was a ghost town, except for the prostitutes and homeless who gathered around barrel fires under the abandoned West Side Highway. Taxicabs refused to take fares there, and local wits claimed that a drunk who passed out on Spring Street at dusk would not get run over until the first garbage trucks rolled out before dawn.

*Inset right: Rip Hayman, homesteader in the House since 1973.*

*Above: Paco in the Ear boudoir.*

*Opposite page: "James Brown Mandala" (1979) by Sari Dienes, made of from shards excavated in the cellar.*

*Below: George Peck, Elder Statesman of the Ear Inn.*

In 1973, a Columbia University student named Rip Hayman was scouring the more obscure reaches of lower Manhattan in search of a cheap, interesting place to live. He finally stumbled upon the seedy, no-name bar on far west Spring Street. Its upper stories were obviously and enticingly vacant:

> *The upstairs windows were broken. I went into the bar, and all these old sailors and longshoremen looked at me as if to say, "where's this kid coming from?" It was more or less their private club. Nobody young or female was allowed in. I kept going back and bugging Joe, the bartender. "Don't bother me," he would say. And he wouldn't serve me. There was only one kind of beer [Rheingold] and three bottles of whiskey on the bar. But I caught the owner once, an old Hungarian man named Harry Jacobs. I kept bugging him to rent me the upstairs and told him I could fix it up. He finally showed it to me; it was filled with junk, and there were holes in the roof. He agreed to rent it to me for $100 a month.*

Rip cleaned out decades worth of junk from the second and third floor rooms and began to make them habitable, even adding bathing facilities. He shared his tilting quarters with a succession of roommates excited by the prospect of living well beyond the frontier of civilized life in the city. Paco Underhill remembers the long winters with barely any heat. They only had a small wood stove on each floor, and to feed them they had to go scavenging for firewood in the surrounding neighborhood

Another outsider who discovered the Green Door was George Peck, now an Ear Inn bartender, who moved into area in the mid-1970s: "It was basically the only bar around, except for Dave's on Canal Street. Inside, it was like a Bowery bar, low lit, dirty, a bum bar." The Green Door's peculiar charms also lured Martin Sheridan, an Irish-born rock music impresario who had opened a rehearsal space

**Ear Upstairs.**
*Clockwise:*

The old kitchen above the bar and the second floor roof deck.

Kitchen fireplace with draft horse shoe found in the chimney.

Stairs to the third floor guest quarters of the House.

The second floor parlor above the Ear Inn bar. The spruce plank floors and fireplace are originals from 1817.

Roof deck over the Ear Inn dining room.

in a semi-abandoned loft building in nearby Tribeca. When his bands finished practicing in the early hours of the morning, he would bring them over for a few drinks and a glimpse of local color:

> *We would go into the Green Door at 5 a.m. It was the low end of the longshoremen's bars, it couldn't get any lower. There would be sixty guys lined up at the bar. It was dark, with curtains over the front windows, full of smoke, and the only light came from a few fluorescent bulbs. A good gust of wind was the best cleaning the bar ever got, and you always checked your chair before you sat down on it. The drinks were awful beer, whiskey and vodka; we always had a beer and a shot like they did. The atmosphere was dour, so out of respect we were dour too. We never talked to any of the regulars, and at the first sign of trouble we got out of there.*

*Above: "Ear", a 1942 painting by Sari Dienes.*

*Opposite: The artist Sari Dienes in 1983, when she was owner of the Ear Inn and Queen of the Bar.*

One of Rip's roommates was Sari Dienes, an artist who through sheer force of personality broached the first crack in the Green Door's inscrutable culture. Born in Hungary in 1898, she had come to the City shortly before World War II, becoming known as "the doyenne of avant-garde New York." Her works ranged from assemblages of found objects to earthworks, happenings and other exciting but ephemeral forms of art. She took no guff from a bunch of drunken, longshoremen, and before long she was propped up at the bar having long conversations with Harry Jacobs. When the regulars asked, "Who is this woman?" Jacobs replied, "This isn't a woman, this is my friend." He had finally found someone who could speak Hungarian with him, who revived memories of his homeland. Eventually the barflies learned to tolerate Dienes, calling her "Phyllis" because her shock of white hair and wild clothes reminded them of the comedienne Phyllis Diller.

In 1977, Harry Jacobs took Rip aside and offered to sell him the bar. The longtime bartender, Joe Romano, had retired after fifty years, and without him Harry could no longer take the daily grind of the business. Rip, Sari Dienes and

*Above: For decades, the neon sign in front of the Ear Inn flashed "BAR." To avoid Landmarks review for any new sign, the ends of the "B" were painted over to rename the pub once only known as the "Green Door." The new name came from the "Ear" music magazine published upstairs from 1975 to 1992.*

*Below: A House bottle holds a doll's carved wooden arm.*

*Opposite left: Whiskey jug unearthed in the cellar., sold whiskey to ships on the nearby docks.*

Paco Underhill had a conference and realized they had to either buy in or be evicted by a new owner. Despite their total lack of business experience, they decided to buy the bar. They had no money, so Sari sold a Robert Rauschenberg painting given to her by the artist, and suddenly the seedy waterfront saloon was theirs. "It was like living in a Mickey Rooney movie," recalls Paco, "Hey, kids, let's open a bar!"

They tore out the linoleum flooring, painted the walls for the first time in at least fifty years and, much to the displeasure of the remaining waterfront mob, removed the jukebox and pool table from the back room. In the backroom, they discovered a kitchen whose previous chef had quit in a hurry about forty years earlier, judging from the fossilized slop-stew still on the stove. Buried in the dirt basement floor were glass bottles and ceramic jugs for beer and whiskey dating back to the Thomas Cloke era. The bar's first chairs and tables were salvaged from the street; for tablecloths they tore squares of paper from huge rolls they scavenged from a nearby printing plant. Rather than go through the red tape required by the Landmarks Preservation Commission to change the facade, Rip used a few strokes of a paintbrush to transform the neon BAR sign out front into EAR—hence the origin of the Ear Inn. It opened officially—with no liquor served—on Thanksgiving Day of 1977.

Rip, Paco and Sari were soon investigated by the State Liquor Authority, bullied by liquor salesmen and threatened by local gangsters. Employees either stole them blind or were too rigorously honest, refusing to give the free drinks that build goodwill. The waiters and

Left: Bar sign from the Thomas Cloke era surrounded by more recent additions.

Right: Above the Ear bar stands a line of ancient bottles excavated from the back cellar.

waitresses, mostly local artists, seemed to take pleasure in ignoring customers and adhered to an unspoken rule against smiling. The French artist-chef Jean Dupuy was temperamental and so slow in producing the food that they put crayons on the table so that diners could amuse themselves while waiting (beginning a custom that countless restaurants across the country have copied). In turn, the staff also had problems with the owners. George Peck, who drifted into the job as bartender, frequently had to pay the waitstaff out of his own pocket. Offended by the higher prices, bohemian atmosphere and the sight of women (and sometimes even children!) in their beloved saloon, the last old regulars left for more traditional (read: grittier) bars in the neighborhood.

Above: The actress Mizuo Peck in 1978.

# Rita
## by Paco Underhill 1981

It was Rita the bartender who told me at the tail end of a heart to heart on garlic sandwiches and cigars. If you've got a run down bar and restaurant on the edge of urban nowhere, the news of a new tenant in the under-populated office building across the street is a small piece of manna from heaven. I'd spent too many lunch hours sitting at the bar munching my tuna fish and watching the cook and the waitress chain smoke cigarettes and read romance novels. The noon hours needed a kick in the pants.

Rita was a California girl, with a mane of brown curls, a ready smile and the arithmetic of a third grader. A personal stake in making sure the cash register tallied out taught her more in two weeks about adding and subtracting than twelve years of Los Angeles public education. I'd hired her on a rainy afternoon after watching her handle Irving Adler, our 82 year old curmudgeon. Irving was an institution who'd been slopping up brandy at the same stool since 1923. Rita had walked in for a beer or to get out of the rain, and three-quarters blind Irving had no trouble seeing she was female and propositioned her on the spot. Irving at 98 pounds, of which 98% was residual Hennessey, was no threat. Rita beamed and with the ease of an experienced gerontologist, not only had him telling stories I'd never heard before, but got him to spring for a beer. The last lady I'd had working the day shift couldn't cope with the dregs of humanity passed on to us by the former owners. She was also so inept at stealing that even I could spot it.

Rita had charm, was even newer than I to the gin-mill trade. She was offered the job and started working sixty seconds later. The customers taught her how to mix the drinks, and making change was her on-the-job training. Toots Shor might not have approved but it worked out just fine until the garlic sandwiches and cigars.

Garlic is a wonderful spice. The benefits have been lauded from Bram Stoker to Adele Davis. I like garlic bread and garlic baked with chicken. I used to eat it toasted on little grills at Korean drinking houses in Seoul. Nonetheless in any form of intimate contact, it takes two garlic eaters to click.

Rita had gone for garlic with a vengeance because of a wonderful film that had passed through town called "Garlic is as Good as Ten Mothers", directed and produced by Les Blank. Rita had talked the cook into making her toasted garlic on whole wheat sandwiches for lunch. Rita's antidote for the after taste was a Cuban cigar. She had found a box of smuggled Havanas behind the bar that previous owners of our dive had traded for drinks with a Canadian trucker. Time and a gradual change in clientele had made that box and a bottle of Rock and Rye the truly slow movers on the back shelf.

The first time it happened I was as amused as everyone else to see Rita in her lime green tank top and electric blue pedal pushers puffing away. She was not Gertude Stein, but looked more like a refugee from a pajama party destined to spend an hour or two clutching the toilet bowl. Her stomach fortified with the garlic sandwiches made no such protest however. The novelty became an everyday habit.

Finally, I had to step in. I pointed out that we were in business together. She sold my drinks and made tips. Anything that helped sell drinks within reason was good business. Anything that drove customers out hurt both of us. While the vision of an attractive young lady chewing on a stogy might add to her tips occasionally, as a standard routine it was not a great idea. Rita got the message.

Despite our garlic sandwich confrontation, Rita had settled into the job with her own brand of logic. When the air-conditioning broke down she'd tend bar in a one piece bathing suit. Our male patrons were appreciative of the view, and Rita's lack of self-consciousness made it seem the most practical and simple of solutions to the heat. She had a wonderful collection of '50's rhinestone sunglasses which were modeled with great aplomb both by Rita and the line up of retired longshoremen, taxi drivers and warehouse men that made up much of our daytime bar trade. She also found a pink high heel shoe large enough to hold the phone. She claimed it made it easier to grab without looking, and that it fit comfortably into her shoulder, freeing both hands as she made Kamikaze gimlets.

Rita lived on the Lower East Side, sharing an apartment with Victor, a very distinguished looking gay black man studying to be a dancer. At her suggestion, we'd hired him to bus tables and wash dishes. The trouble started in Rita's apartment on the Lower East Side when in the course of a weekend she and Victor swapped boy friends. God knows the circumstances or how long the exchange had been in the making. In the cramped tenement rooms of that part of town, you get as intimate with your neighbors as you can with a Siamese twin.

It had not been an amiable trade, and the drama of the weekend spilled over into Monday afternoon. It began as muttered words on betrayal, slippery seduction, and unnatural penetration. It quickly degenerated into a cross fire of dirty dishes from one direction and dirty glasses from the other. Caught in the middle was the table of ladies from across the street. As the accuracy diminished it was clear the two of them were venting more than their frustration with each other. It was bedlam. The feminist art ladies from across the street switched their afternoon club house to the Greek diner down the street.

Rita and her roommate made peace, but made a point of not working the same hours. Victor quit about two months after the end of the club house to become a window dresser. I gathered too that he and Rita were no longer sharing an apartment. The swapped boy friends didn't last long, and after a while Rita finally picked a favorite from her fans on the afternoon shift. She approached romance with exuberance of a large puppy. Kurt, a dispatcher for a taxi company, was round-faced with a mop of black hair, dark eyes and the recipient of her affections. He was met every time he opened the bar room door with her flying body and loud wet kisses. She nicknamed him Baby, and most of us forgot his real name.

Baby was a hollow leg drinker. A fifth of vodka would do no more than put a spot of color in his cheek. Thank god he was a taxi dispatcher rather than a driver. He took his role as the darling of the daytime queen with good grace, not taking advantage of his position to become a free loader as often happens with the girl and boy friends of people who work in bars. The crew from the taxi company also became a group of regulars, and Baby policed their language and manners with an iron fist.

Through this period Rita begun to grow out of her California flakiness. Some of the change I attribute to the other members of our staff. Between the poets washing dishes and the classically trained actors and actresses waiting tables, we had enough doctorates and masters degrees on the floor to open a liberal arts college. One of the dish washers gave two weeks notice and said he'd been named to the American Academy in Rome. Another bartender quit after having accepted a screen writer's job in L.A. She specialized in horror movies, and at this writing has a couple major screen credits under her belt. While I was barely making a living, I was proud and touched by the extended family of characters dependent on the gin mill for their rent money. For Rita the atmosphere was conducive to change. One sleepy afternoon I walked in to find her sprawled out on her elbows across the empty bar with a dictionary and Plato's Dialogues. She'd taken to wearing her bushy hair in a pony tail on the left side of her head.

Rita switched over to working nights and picked a up a part time job painting door frames on Wall Street with a contracting firm. She'd come to work with a delicate spattering of paint across her face.

Rita's quitting was traumatic. Baby left the bar one evening with one of his buddies, neither of them feeling any pain. Outside the bar they found a man sitting on the hood of their car reading a newspaper. Baby in good jocular humor asked the man to remove himself, and a fight broke out. Windows were broken and Rita called the cops. I walked in minutes after to find Rita in tears. Loyalty towards the bar and concern for our windows had made her bring the police down on her Baby. I took over and finished her shift as she chased after her boyfriend.

I didn't see her again for some months. The trauma of having abdicated her throne obviously took time to work out. At last meeting she was working in fashion, looking wonderful, but I detected under her perfume the faint smell of garlic.

# 10th Anniversary Special Issue

MAGAZINE EAST

*New Wilderness Foundation, Inc.*
*325 Spring Street Room 208*
*New York, New York 10013*

**Volume 8, Number 1–2**
**February/March/April/May 1983**
**$4.00 (U.S. Dollars)**

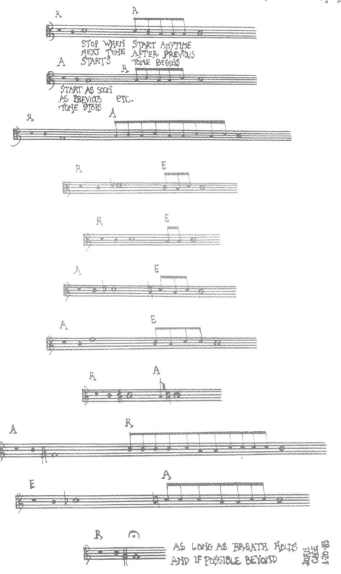

The Ear Inn nevertheless slowly began to attract a dedicated following. A feminist artists' group whose offices were across the street made the Ear their hangout—until they were caught in the middle of a dish-throwing fight between two waiters. Rip organized avant-garde events that attracted artists and musicians, including John Lennon, Mike Bloomfield, Tom Waites, John Cage and Laurie Anderson. The earliest poetry readings were staged by a group of Village-Voice-deliverymen-cum-poets who made the Ear their watering hole. At their first performance, a competing group of poets tried to scare away the audience with baseball bats. The Ear's poetry series is the second oldest in the city, and has featured luminaries such as Allen Ginsberg and John Ashberry among the readers. The Ear's

*Above: Cabaret in the newly opened Ear Inn in 1978.*

*Opposite: Ear Magazine cover by John Cage. The new music journal was published from 1973 to 1992 in California and New York editions, the eastern edition beginning in the upstairs of the House.*

*Above: Neighborhood view from Pier 40 Hudson River.*

greatest attraction was its inclusiveness. Unlike the old Green Door, the Ear welcomed everybody, not just local workmen and neighbors but artists, lawyers, society girls, movie stars, taxicab drivers and students. In a city where everything has an angle, people found the Ear's democratic atmosphere refreshing, and the bar began to thrive

## Where are we?

This neighborhood-between-others has been variously described over the years as:

**Twin Springs**
when the area was bordered by marshes, Minetta and Collect streams

**Calk Hook**
when there was a white spit of land near Canal St.

**Lispenard Meadows**
when the Lispenards farmed

**the Upper West Side**
when the city was downtown

**the Lower West Side**
when the city was uptown

**Lower Greenwich**

**South Village**

**NoCal**
(north of Canal)

**Hudson Square**
(where is the square?)

**HDYGTDHT—**
(HowDoYaGetToDaHollandTunnel?)

**West Soho**

**Woho**

**SoWha**

IN NEW YORK CITY

# JAMES BROWN HOUSE

EAR * INN * VIRONS

E
N ⊙ S
W

6TH AVE

VARICK ST

HUDSON ST

RENWICK ST

GREENWICH ST

SPRING ST

dominick St

Prince St

Holland Tunnel

CANAL ST

JAMES BROWN HOUSE
EAR INN

WATTS ST

WASHINGTON St

CANAL STREET PARK

WEST St (westside Hwy)

W HOUSTON ST

PIER 40

HUDSON RIVER PARK

PIER 32

HUDSON RIVER

TRIBECA BASIN

Adams

*Map by Lisa Adams*

*Above: A view of later day life in the Ear Inn by Jillian Slattery.*

*Opposite right: Six taps, a spare stool and some slack time in a busy town. This one's for you. (with Gary Lawler in motion)*

By the early 1980s, Rip and Paco grew weary of cigarette smoke blown in their faces every night, and Sari, now in her mid eighties, lacked the energy to be the Queen of the Bar. Back in 1978, Rip had assumed 326 Spring's title and mortgage from Hermine Chanin, a descendant of Ethel Nussdorf. Now Rip, Sari and Paco wanted to find a new owner for the Ear Inn who would maintain the bar's non-conformist traditions. They heard that Martin Sheridan and Gerard Walker, both occasional patrons of the Ear, might be interested. Martin had grown up in his family's pub in Ireland, knew the tavern from Green Door days and understood the unique essence of the Ear Inn. Jerry had restaurant management experience and from his first glimpse of the Ear operation knew immediately that something needed fixing: "It seemed like the bar was being run by committee and that they did everything they could to discourage business."

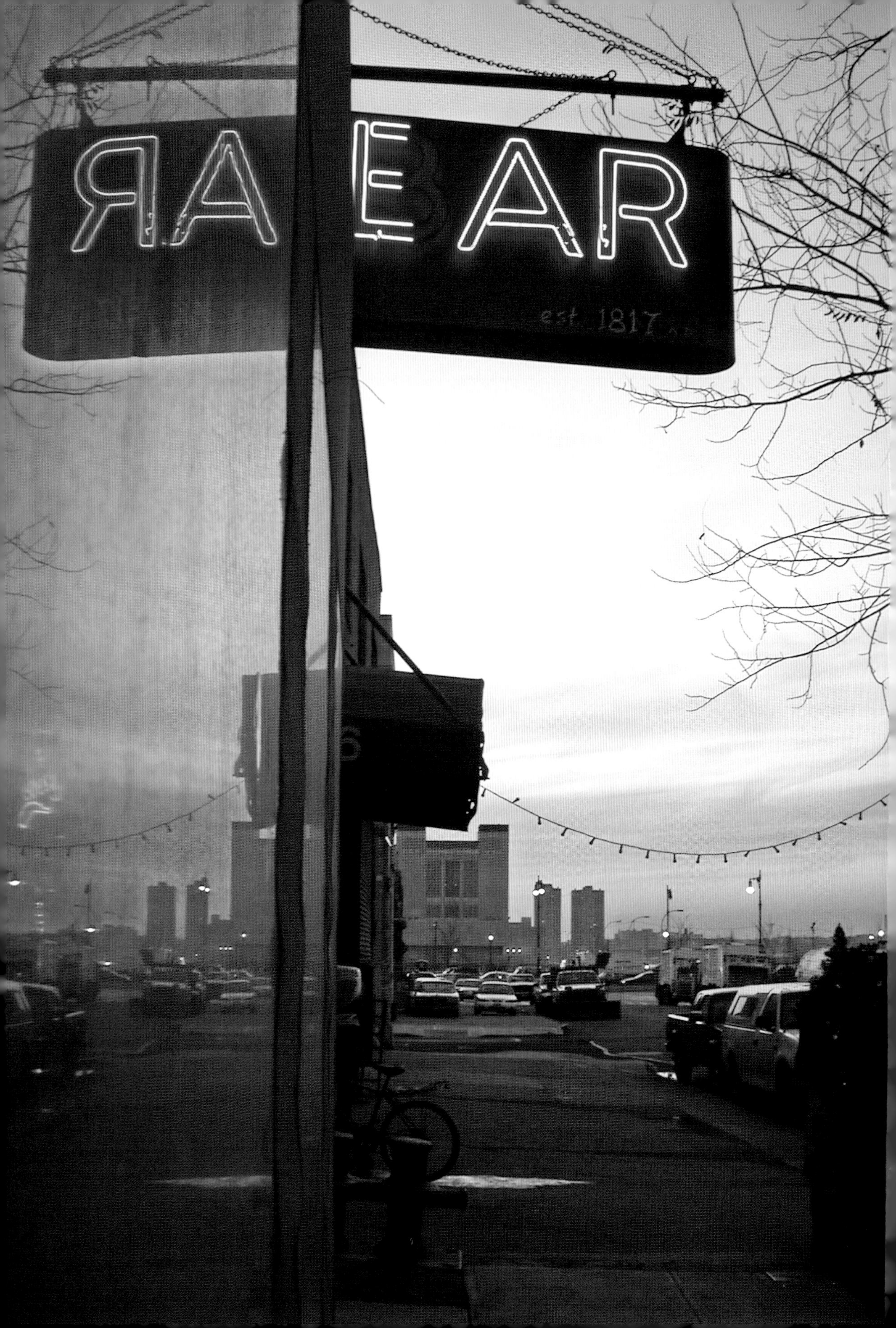
est. 1817

# JAMES BROWN HOUSE

## "More like it used to be, than it ever was...."

**Overheard about the Ear:**

*Intimate, charmingly seedy and evocative of another century.*
—Newsday Magazine, 1982

*A dump with dignity...*
—NY Times, 1994

*Last of the neighborhood places...*
—George Peck, Downtown Express, 1995

**Chinese acupuncture chart**

*What a friendy bar! They even know their ghost by name.*
—Daily News, 1996

*A breeding ground of urban myths.*
—Kate Sekules, New York Magazine, 1997

*The House relies on the kindness of neighbors for structural and spiritual support.*
—David Firestone, NY Times, 1998

*The neighborhood-in-all-but-name's defining institution.*
—Doug Cooper, NY Times 2000

*Garnering the endearment of poets and plumbers alike, the crowd at the Ear is eclectic on the verge of miscellaneous, yet utterly at ease with its disparities.*
—Melissa Robbins, Downtown Express, 2000

*The antithesis of slick... seafarers in need of divey relief and homemade grub call it a great place to have one more and beg all to lend an ear.*
—Zagat Survey, 2001

*"...the ceilings are not too low for a stunted bow legged seadog ... kept dark to protect the innocent."*
—NY Sun, 2002

*As long as the Chinese don't drink and the Irish don't cook, this place will last forever...*
—La Zi

*"The weakest ink outlives the strongest memory."—Confucius*

Martin and Jerry bought the Ear Inn business from Rip, Paco and Sari and immediately began to make some changes. "We asked the staff to be kind to the people they were serving," said Jerry, "to smile at them now and then. We bought drinks for people; we were friendly to them".

*Above: Martin Sheridan and Gerard Walker, publicans par excellance.*

*Opposite right: "View Out of the Ear", painting of Tevia Ito by Harry McCormick, 1978*

It took the new owners two years to get the business on a sound footing. Most of the old, cantankerous employees moved on to fame and fortune in other venues (George Peck is the last survivor of the early, eccentric days). Martin and Jerry would fix a pipe and another would break; Jerry frequently found himself behind the stove while Martin washed the dishes. At the same time, they managed to preserve the bar's unique atmosphere and build its clientele without losing the old customers. Martin and Jerry still run the Ear Inn almost two decades later and continue to preserve and improve upon the groundwork laid by its heritage of publicans.

### RECONSTRUCTION UPDATE

*The House was extensively renovated in 1999-2001 with a new roof, windows and stonework repairs, made possible with finance from the Historic Properties Fund of the New York Landmark Conservancy.*

The James Brown House has survived in its obscure corner of Manhattan Island for over 180 years. For most of that time, its neighborhood was a dumping ground for whatever the rest of Manhattan did not want, including slaughterhouses, lumberyards, factories, tunnel entrances, garbage trucks and thousands of new immigrants. But when a disparate group of architectural historians, students and artists realized that 326 Spring Street was a gem from the city's past, something changed. Not only was the building restored with finance assistence from the NY Landmarks Conservancy, but due to its benevolent presence, people suddenly wanted to live on far west Spring Street again. As human scale and rising real estate prices return to the neighborhood, the James Brown House faces a whole new set of challenges for survival into its third century.

*The arched roadway Canal St. Bridge was at its contruction in the 1920's one of the largest of its kind. It was torn down in the early 1980's, despite proposals by engineers to move the bridge. The community opposed the Westway Interstate plan to fill in the river to the pier heads and make a tunneled route along the shore. Today car traffic has returned to the waterfront with the construction of Route 9A and Hudson River Park.*

**Memory of Pastscapes**

*The waterfront in the 1980's with Barbara Pollitt on Pier 36, now the Tribeca Basin ecological preserve.*

*Above: West Side Highway demolition in progress. Right: Corner of Spring and Washington Streets on 9/11/2001 at 8:59 in the morning. The World Trade Center "Big Brothers" loomed over the Lower West Side for 26 years, a monumental presence that was taken for granted until September 2001. On that fateful day, the James Brown House was coated from the dust of the collapse 10 blocks south. The Ear Inn lost many friends, yet stayed open for the aftermath week, passing out all its supplies, and serving as a place of respite for the police, fire and rescue teams, and the Army National Guard which camped on the block.*

# THE EAR INN

**Live Music**

Monday,
Tuesday,
Wednesday

11:00 pm - 4:00 am

**Lunch & Dinner**

Daily
12:00 pm - 1:00 am

**Poetry Reading**

Saturday 3:00 pm

## . . . 326 SPRING STREET, N.Y.C 10013

212 - 226 - 9060

**James Brown House**—A New York Icon
ISBN: 962-217-718-2

First edition 2002 © James Brown House LLC in cooperation with Odyssey Guides,
an imprint of Airphoto International Ltd., Hong Kong.

**Credits:**
Text: Andrew Coe
Editor: Albert LaFarge
Design: Anne Lawrence
Map: Lisa Lyman Adams
Archive and digital restoration: Lou Scrima

**Photos:**
Herbert Taylor
New York Historical Society
Museum of the City of New York
Metropolitan Museum
Paco Underhill

Chris Craig
Rip Hayman
Tom Rush
David Paler
Anne Lawrence

Printed in China by Twin Age Ltd. E-mail: twinage@netvigator.com

**Distributed in the United States by W.W. Norton & Company, Inc.
500 Fifth Avenue, New York, NY 10110, Tel: (800) 233-4830, Fax: (800) 458-6515**

Thanks to the Friends of the James Brown House:

Christo
Catharina Cosin
Paco Underhill
Barbara Pollitt
Ken Sugarman
Robert Polifka
Carl Schwartz
Ben Kursman
Dion Drislane
Dr. B.C. Vermeersch
Steve O'Rouke
Sean O'Rouke
Liam O'Connor
Gary Lawler
John Griffin
Jack O'Reilly
William Royce Webb
Kate Webb
Kathy Barbieri
John Seminario
Chi DiMaggio
Clay Jackson
Erika Sipos
Mark Sweeney
David Lawrence
Ned Sublette
Jon & Joanne Hendricks
Geoff Hendricks
Don Hill
Susan LaRosa
Christopher Gray

Dr. Sherril Wilson,
   African Burial Ground
Pierre & Coleen Cournot
Queva Lutz
Jeff Hewitt
Christine Lehner
Capt. George Pesicola
Capt. Jim Gallagher
Cynthia Adams
Nina Lundborg
Vivienne LaMothe
Pam Jarvis
Charlie Morrow
Ludovica Villar-Hauser
Victor Villar
John Paul
Joe Haske
Ed Masler
Cecily Brown
Susan Brown
Andrea Brown
Pooh Kaye
Conrad Vogel
Mablen Jones
David Leith
Elizabeth Comerford
Dr. Harold Fogstad
Pauline Oliveros
Kipp & Margot Osborne
Burt Migdal
Tom Fox

Richard Barrett
Carole DeSaram,
   Tribeca Community Assoc.
Katherine Freed
Aubrey Lees
Alan Gerson
Tom Duane
Dave Reck
Arthur Imperatore, Sr. & Jr.
Nancy Hardy
John Caime
John Marshall
Kim Valente, Landmarks
   Preservation Commission
Kent Barwick
Tim Lynch, P.E.
   Robert Silman Associates
Tim Allenbrook, AIA
Landmarks Conservancy:
   Roger Lang, Karen Anzis,
   Andrea Goldwyn
Preserv, Inc.: Carl Culbreth,
   Brian Lyle and crew
Englander Millwork
Nino Vendome
Nat and Fran Plotkin
Larry Caputo
Del Geist
Patricia Leighton
Jessica Goodyear
Stephane Pagani

Savannah
Harvey Simon
Magnus Bartlett
Andy Forget
Doug and Eliza Rice
Alexander Stewart
John Ventinegila
Michael Imperoli
John Ford
James Gandolfini
David Byrne
Joe Jackson
John Lennon and Yoko Ono
George Peck and family
Kevin Hackett
Paul O'Brian
Seamus South
Mike Shelhan (CH 5)
David Diaz (CH 2)
Frank Dowd
Chris Spring
Marty Holland
Jim O'Conner
Michael Rogol
Lauren Rowland
Tom Rossi
Ulysses Sheridan
Stanley
Chef Tommy Wong and the
   Ear kitchen crew
and all the Ear Regulars......

**Other Icon books from Odyssey Publications:** Icon Series conceived by Magnus Bartlett

**N.Y.P.D—a History**—in association with the Police Museum
**F.D.N.Y—an illustrated History**—in association with the Fire Department Museum
**George Washington**—in association with Mt. Vernon Historical Site
**Gold Fever**—in association with the Oakland Museum
**Civil War Soldier**—in association with the Pamplin Park Museum

For even more infomation: Ear Inn: 212-226-9060 James Brown House 212-219-8026
www.jamesbrownhouse.com / www.earinn.com / magnusb@netvigator.com / www.wwnorton.com